Syria and the Assad Family: The History Behind Power and the Civil War

By Charles River Editors

About Charles River Editors

Charles River Editors was founded by Harvard and MIT alumni to provide superior editing and original writing services, with the expertise to create digital content for publishers across a vast range of subject matter. In addition to providing original digital content for third party publishers, Charles River Editors republishes civilization's greatest literary works, bringing them to a new generation via ebooks.

Introduction

A billboard in Damascus of Assad with the words "God protects Syria"

Bashar al-Assad (1965-)

"I'm not a puppet. I wasn't made by the west to go to the west or any other country. I'm Syrian. I'm made in Syria. I have to live in Syria and die in Syria." – Bashar al-Assad, 2012

In early 2011, a political movement swept across the Arabic speaking world that toppled despotic regimes and dictatorships. The political movement, which became known as the "Arab Spring," was popular in nature and made use of the internet, particularly social networking websites, to remove dictators such as Ben Ali of Tunisia, Hosni Mubarak of Egypt, and Muammar Qadaffi of Libya. Those dictators, who ruled their countries for decades, were unable to stem the tide of popular indignation against them even though they tried using force and propaganda in ways reminiscent of the Cold War era.

While some of these dictators bowed to the political pressure and others were pushed out by force through civil wars, the events of the Arab Spring have come to be overshadowed by the civil war in the Arabic speaking nation of Syria, which has been ruled throughout the 21st century by Bashar al-Assad. Though he had not planned on ruling Syria, several events conspired to make Bashar the successor of his father Hafez, who himself was notorious for crushing an uprising in the Syrian city of Hama by massacring thousands of inhabitants. Though the West frequently looked for signs that Bashar might be a reformer, due in part to his formerly popular Western wife, Assad remained part of a critical alliance with Iran and the sub-state groups Hamas and Hezbollah, forming an influential bloc that has influenced events across the Middle

East, and one that Israel and the West have tried to break over the past decade.

Like the other dictators, Assad faced popular demonstrations against his regime at the height of the Arab Spring, but the outcome has proved to be much different there than in the other Arab nations. Assad steadfastly refused to step down from power, and the protests against him and his government quickly turned violent, which eventually enveloped Syria in a civil war that has already killed over 100,000, left over half a million refugees, and shows no signs of ending anytime soon. Furthermore, on August 21, 2013, a chemical weapon attack outside of the capital city Damascus left around 1,500 civilians dead, and anti-Assad factions in Syria, as well as enemies of the Assad regime in other countries, have blamed Bashar for the attack, while Assad claims his enemies are responsible.

A crisis that may have threatened to involve either the United States, Russia, or both, appears to have been solved at least temporarily, but bigger issues concerning Syria still remain. The two major questions that concern the future of Syria are whether Bashar al-Assad will literally and politically survive the civil war, and what Syria's future will be in the wake of the civil war. Answering these questions requires an understanding of Bashar's religious sect, the Alawites, the regional strife among Sunni and Shiite nations, Arab nationalism, and the Assad family as a whole.

Syria and the Assad Family is a history that examines how Hafez al-Assad's middle son grew up and the events that brought him to power in Syria. It also comprehensively analyzes the ongoing civil war against Assad. Along with pictures of important people, places, and events, you will learn about Syria's notorious dictator like you never have before.

Chapter 1: The Alawites and Modern Syrian History

One of the most integral aspects of Bashar al-Assad's background is the religious sect that he and his family belong to, and it's one that explains the root of Syria's civil war. The Alawites are a religious sect whose members come exclusively from four tribes or clans (Seale 1995, 9), but they also have ethnic origins that are unique from the rest of their Syrian Arab neighbors. However, despite the fact they are a religious minority in Syria, comprising about 12-13% of the population in recent decades (Faksh 1984, 134), their power in both the military and the ruling Ba'ath Party has been immense and disproportionate for over half a century.

The Alawites have lived in the northwest region of Syria for centuries, which is mainly mountainous but also contains plains and the major city of Latakia (Nisan 2002, 117), but their ethnic origins are a mystery, even as numerous stories and legends testify to their ancestry. Some legends place their ancestral homeland in Persia, while another far-fetched theory ascribes a group of European Crusaders as the progenitors of their sect (Nisan 2002, 114). A more logical explanation for the ethnic origins of the Alawites is that they descended from an ancient Canaanite tribe that was indigenous to the region and subsequently became an insular culture in their mountainous homeland over the centuries (Faksh 1984, 134).

The mysterious ethnic origins of the Alawites are dwarfed by the even more mysterious origins and theology of their actual religion. The theological origins of the Alawite sect can be traced back to a prophet named Muhammad Ibn Nusair, who in 891 is believed to have seen Jesus (Nissan 2002, 116). Because Nusair is considered the founder of the sect, the Alawites are often referred to as Nusayria; in fact, the name Alawite has only been used as a nomenclature for the sect since the period of French rule in Syria from 1921-1945 (Seale 1995, 9). Today, the Alawites are considered to be from the Shia branch of Islam, particularly derived from the Ishamili sect, which is where they probably first adopted the use of the Arabic language (Faksh 1984, 134). The Alawites share with other Shia Muslims the idea of the importance of Ali, a cousin of Muhammad, but they carry that significance to the point that he is viewed as divine in much the same way as Jesus, a theological view eschewed by other Shias (Nissan 2002, 116).

Other than speaking the language of the prophet Muhammad and technically being Shiite, the Alawites share few other similarities with other Muslims, even other Shiites. There are clearly non-Abrahamic (and probably pagan) influences in Alawite theology, namely the idea of reincarnation (Faksh 1984, 135), which may come from Canaanite roots. Christianity has also influenced the Alawites, who use ceremonial wine and observe Christmas (Faksh 1984, 136). Perhaps the most important aspect of Alawite culture and theology that has influenced their course in history is their practice of secrecy. The Alawite practice of secrecy, known in Arabic as *taqiya*, was adopted to protect them from persecution by other Muslims, but it has had the effect of turning their sect into an esoteric religion that only the initiates truly know and understand (Faksh 1984, 135). Since Alawite theology is so different from the main body of either Sunni or

Shia Islam, it is considered a heterodox sect, and some more conservative Sunni Muslims view them as apostates. The heterodox aspect of the Alawite sect was a major cause for their self-segregation and discrimination at the hands of other Muslims, but it was also what ultimately propelled them to rule over the Syrian state.

In modern times, the fate of the Alawites has never been an easy one. When Syria was ruled by the Ottoman Empire, the predominately Sunni Turkish overlords abused and reviled the Alawites and often enslaved their women and children (Batatu 1981, 334). Because of their physical and social isolation due to their beliefs, the Alawites often comprised the lowest rungs of Syria's socio-economic ladder. The status and treatment that the Alawites received led to their general distrust of outsiders, particularly the Sunnis who comprised the upper rungs of the socio-economic ladder in Syria (Faksh 1984, 135).

The dire and seemingly hopeless situation of the Alawites would change when the Ottoman Empire collapsed after World War I. Since the Ottoman Empire was on the losing side of World War I, it was forced to relinquish its imperial possessions as part of a League of Nations mandate, and temporary control of modern Syria was given to France in 1921, which lasted until the end of World War II. Although the French were not Muslims, the Alawites made great societal progress under their rule, thanks to France's suspicions of the Syrian Sunni elite. In order to mitigate their power, the French limited Sunni influence in the military by creating the Troupes Spéciales, military units comprised primarily of minorities such as the Kurds, Ishmailis, Druze, and most importantly the Alawites (Nisan 2002, 119). In fact, three of eight infantry battalions in the Troupes Spéciales were Alawite (Nissan 2002, 119), and the French encouraged the religious minorities in Syria to join the Troupes Spéciales as a way to counter the nationalist and Islamist tendencies of the Sunni majority, as well as to secure a loyal political base for themselves (Faksh 1984, 143). Due to their social and economic plight, many young Alawite men joined the military because its doors were open to them, whereas so many other economic doors in Syria had long been closed (Seale 1995, 18). Eventually, the Alawites would come to dominate the Syrian military structure.

Chapter 2: Arab Nationalism and the Syrian Ba'ath Party

Membership in the Alawite sect played a role in the eventual rise to power of the Assad family, but it was a religion that they were born into. Similarly, Syrian identity politics was something that they were forced to identify with. However, their membership in the Ba'ath Party was much more calculated and demonstrated the political acumen of Bashar's father, Hafez al-Assad.

Hafez al-Assad

The Syrian Ba'ath Party, which would be the ruling party of the Syrian state from the 1960s until the present, represented a unique form of nationalism that became popular in the Middle East after World War II. Nationalism was once defined by Ernest Gellner as "a theory of political legitimacy, which requires that ethnic boundaries should not cut across political ones, and, in particular, that ethnic boundaries within a given state – a contingency already formally excluded by the principle in its general formulation – should not separate the power-holders from the rest." (Gellner 1983, 1). Gellner further argued that nationalism is contingent upon the idea of the modern state and thus did not exist in pre-modern times (Gellner 1983, 4). Based on this definition, the philosophical concept of nationalism is essentially a modern 19th century Western idea that originated in such places as France, Germany, and England. The idea of nationalism led to the unification of the Italian speaking kingdoms and city-states into the kingdom of Italy in 1861, and a similar process took place that created the modern German state in 1879.

Although the concept of modern nationalism may have first been articulated in Western Europe, the idea spread to many regions that were either ruled outright by or heavily influenced by colonial European powers. After World War II, a wave of Arab nationalism swept across the Middle East that was promulgated by intellectuals in parlors and universities and advocated in the streets. In its early manifestation, Arab nationalism followed most of the same paradigms as European nationalism, which may have been the result of many of the Arab peoples being under the yoke of European colonialism, but the Arab version also had its own unique nuances. At its core, Arab nationalism stood for the political unity of all Arabic speaking peoples – from Morocco to Iraq – because without the idea of political unity it "would be a creed without a purpose, indeed without a meaning (Dawisha 2003, 1)."

However, theory and practice are often two entirely different things, and that was often the case with Arab nationalism. Regional and petty rivalries often formed barriers to the ultimate goal, and the Arab world also seemed to lack a forceful and charismatic leader who could put the idea of nationalism into action.

For a time, the void of an Arab leader in the post-World War II Middle East who epitomized the values of Arab nationalism came to be filled, at least temporarily, by Egyptian president Gamal Abdel Nasser. Gamal Nasser (1918-1970) was part of a *coup d'état* that overthrew Farouk, the king of Egypt, in 1952. Nasser became prime minister of Egypt that year, but due to his ambitious nature he overthrew Muhammad Neguib in 1954 and became president, and essentially dictator, of the country until his death (Wright 2006, 443). From the beginning, Nasser became a global lightning-rod as he stood up to the Western powers of Great Britain, France, and Israel during the Suez Canal Crisis in 1956 and fought wars against Israel in 1956 and 1967 (Wright 2006, 443). Nasser moved his country towards closer relations with the Soviet Union during his reign by accepting aid in the form of military supplies and engineers who helped the Egyptians build the Aswan Dam (Wright 2006, 443). All of these actions by Nasser raised the ire of Western nations, including the United States, but they made him a hero in the eyes of the Arabic speaking world. Nasser may not have won all of his battles against the West and Israel, but he was willing to take the fight to them and speak for those who felt they had no voice.

Nasser waving to a crowd

Besides the direct actions he took, Nasser was also an accomplished public speaker who articulated a version of Arab nationalism that gained adherents in many countries, including Syria. In one of his speeches, Nasser spelled out the roots of Arab nationalism:

> "Can we ignore that there is a Muslim world with which we are tied by bonds which are not only forged by religious faith but also tightened by the facts of history? I said once that fate plays no jokes. It is not in vain that our country lies to the southwest of Asia, close to the Arab world, whose life is intermingled with ours. It is not in vain that our country lies to the northeast of Africa, a position from which it gives upon the dark continent wherein rages today the most violent struggle between white colonizers and black natives for the possession of its inexhaustible resources. It is not in vain that Islamic civilization and Islamic heritage, which the Mongols ravaged in their conquest of the old Islamic capitals, retreated, and sought refuge in Egypt, where they found shelter and safety as a result of the counterattack with which Egypt repelled the invasion of these Tartars at Ein Galout." (Nasser 1962, 230)

Although Nasser's nationalist views took a decidedly Egyptian-centric stance, his words and deeds influenced many across the Arab world to take a similar course. One man who was influenced by and followed the path of Nasser was a Syrian named Michel Aflaq. Aflaq believed in Arab nationalism, like Nasser, but unlike Nasser and most Arabs, Aflaq was a Christian (Seale 1995, 31). Despite being a devout Greek Orthodox, Aflaq still believed that Islam held many virtues, but he viewed Islam as being more of a culture that united Arabs regardless of faith than as a religion (Seale 1995, 31). Due at least in part to his Christian background, Aflaq's brand of Arab nationalism stressed the importance of the Arabs as a race who share a common spirit more so than any common religion. Aflaq wrote:

> "Nationalism is racial in the sense that we hold sacred this Arab race which has, since the earliest historical epochs, carried within itself a vitality and a nobility which have enabled it to go on renewing and perfecting itself, taking advantage of triumphs and defeats alike. Nationalism is spiritual and all-embracing, in the sense that it opens its arms to and spreads its wings over all those who have shared with the Arabs their history and have lived in the environment of their language and culture for generations, so that they have become Arab in thought and feeling. There is no fear that nationalism will clash with religion, for, like religion, it flows from the heart and issues from the will of God." (Aflaq 1962, 243)

Aflaq (right) with Iraqi President Ahmad Hasan al-Bakr, 1968

Aflaq eventually formulated a political program to turn his ideas from theory into reality by coming up with the idea of a political party that would draw from existing groups of young Syrian nationalists (Dawisha 2003, 80). This party became known as the Ba'ath Party, and it was officially founded in 1947 in Damascus, Syria by Aflaq and several other young nationalists who wished to create one Arab nation-state (Dawisha 2003, 124-25). The Ba'ath Party was explicit that although it was based in Syria, it believed that the entire Arab speaking world should be unified as one nation-state; the party's foundation charter states:

> 1) The Arab fatherland constitutes an indivisible political and economic unity. No Arab country can live apart from the others. 2) The Arab nation constitutes a cultural unity. Any differences existing among its sons are accidental and unimportant. They will all disappear with the awakening of the Arab consciousness. 3) The Arab fatherland belongs to the Arabs. They alone have the right to administer its affairs, to dispose of its wealth, and to direct its destinies. (Arab Ba'ath Party 1962, 233)

The Ba'ath Party was also undeniably anti-colonialist, no doubt as a result of Syria's experience as an Ottoman colony and as part of the French Mandate. The party also favored socialism in the economic realm, and even though Ba'ath Party socialism was not of the communist variety being practiced in the Soviet Union, it was still an economic theory that promoted economic equity among its citizens. Concerning Arab socialism, the charter said:

> *Article 4* The Party of the Arab Ba'th is a socialist party. It believes that socialism is a necessity which emanates from the depth of Arab nationalism itself. Socialism constitutes, in fact, the ideal social order which will allow the Arab people to realize its possibilities and to enable its genius to flourish, and which will ensure for the nation constant progress in its material and moral output. It makes possible a trustful brotherhood among its members. (Arab Ba'ath Party 1962, 235)

The Syrian Ba'ath Party eventually diffused outside of Syria, most notably to Iraq (Dawisha 2003, 155-56), but in Syria it provided the framework for the government from the 1960s until the present. The Alawites entered the Ba'ath Party for many of the same reasons they entered the military: doors were often closed to them in other parties. The Ba'ath Party espoused a secular ideology that was appealing to the Alawites because it helped to free them from their minority status and place them on equal footing with the Sunnis (Faksh 1984, 140).

In the early years of the Ba'ath Party, its membership was dominated numerically by Syrians from rural backgrounds and members of the Ishmaili, Druze, and Alawite sects (Faksh 1984, 141). The Alawite dominance in the military and Ba'ath Party would eventually make Syria a state ruled by a minority group, which is somewhat ironic considering the background of the Alawites and the fact that the Ba'ath Party professes to be an Arab nationalist party.

Chapter 3: Hafez al-Assad and the Establishment of the Assad Dynasty

The immense power that Bashar al-Assad currently wields is the direct result of Hafez al-Assad's long and Machiavellian ascent to the presidency of Syria. Hafez was born in 1930 to a poor Alawite family that was originally surnamed Wahhish, but the name was changed by the family patriarch, Ali, in 1927 to Assad (Seale 1995, 6). Ali believed that Assad ("lion" in Arabic) was much more noble than Wahhish, which is best translated into English as "savage" (Seale 1995, 6).

Young Hafez left the cocoon of his Alawite village when he was sent to school in Latakia in 1939, and it was in Latakia that Assad first saw the mistreatment of Alawites at the hands of other Syrians. It was also at this young age that Hafez appears to have realized his life mission. He worked extra hard in school and did well (Seale 1995, 25), which led to his eventual acceptance into the Homs military school (Seale 1995, 39).

Hafez proved to be a good student at Homs and eventually became a pilot (Seale 1995, 59), a position that allowed him to make critical political connections with Ba'ath Party members from across Syrian society (Seale 1995, 60). Much like Hafez witnessed the mistreatment of his fellow Alawites when he first left home, in the military he witnessed how Syria was viewed by other countries in the Arab world while he was in the army. In 1958, the year Hafez married Bashar's mother, Anisa, Syria was joined in political union with Egypt under the leadership of Nasser (Seale 1995, 55). Although this appeared to be the first step in the eventual goal of Arab unity as proposed by Arab nationalists, the reality was quite different for Syria and proved to be a personal burden for Assad. Hafez was sent to a military barracks in Egypt in 1959, where he then witnessed that Syria was a second hand partner in the United Arab Republic (Seale 1995, 60). The United Arab Republic was a logistical nightmare since the two main components, Egypt and Syria, were divided by hundreds of miles, and between them was their archenemy: the state of Israel. The Syrians also felt slighted and thought they were not being treated as equal partners, and the union was dissolved when a military junta took power in Syria in 1961 (Seale 1995, 67-68). Although Assad played no direct role in the *coup d'état* because he was stationed in Egypt at the time, he was placed in an Egyptian jail for 44 days (Seale 1995, 68).

The Assad family. Hafez and Anisa are sitting, and behind them (from left to right) are Maher, Bashar, Basil, Majid, and Bushra.

When Assad returned to Syria, things were much different; the Alawite-controlled military ruled the government and the Ba'ath Party was a growing force. The civil unrest that Syria is now experiencing is nothing new to the country; it was civil unrest in Syria that brought the military to power and ultimately hoisted Hafez into the highest echelons of Syrian power. The military junta that took power in 1961 and split the union with Egypt proved to be only temporary, because another conspiracy within the military soon came to fruition. In March 1963, the government was overthrown once more by members of the military, but this time the soldiers were ardent members of the Ba'ath Party (Seale 1995, 77-78). The Ba'ath Party effectively made Syria a one party state when it ordered Decree #51 on March 9, 1963, which established martial law, and when the dust settled, Hafez was rewarded for his services by being given a presidential cabinet position: defense minister ((Lesch 2012, 71).

The conflicts within Syria helped Hafez rise to power, but it was Syria's conflicts with Israel that solidified his place as place as a genuine Arab ruler. Despite losing the 1948 war against Israel, Arab nations throughout the Middle East had still refused to recognize Israel's right to exist, even as Israel found itself in possession of more land after 1948 than envisioned by the U.N. Partition Plan. Still, the armistice line between Israel and the West Bank (controlled by

Jordan after the 1948 war), known today as the Green Line, still left Israel less than 10 miles wide in some positions. In the summer of 1967, the armies of Jordan and Syria mobilized near Israel's borders, while Egypt's army mobilized in the Sinai Peninsula just west of the Gaza Strip. Combined, the Arab armies numbered over 200,000 soldiers.

In early June 1967, the Israelis captured Jordanian intelligence that indicated an invasion was imminent, and on June 5, the Israelis launched a preemptive attack that knocked out the air forces of its Arab neighbors. Over the next six days, the Israelis overwhelmed the Egyptians in the west, destroying thousands of tanks and capturing the Gaza Strip and the entire Sinai Peninsula. At the same time, Israel drove the Jordanians out of Jerusalem and the West Bank, and it captured the Golan Heights from Syria near the border of Lebanon. In the span of a week, Israel had tripled the size of the lands it controlled. Israel had gone from less than 10 miles wide in some spots to over 200 miles wide from the Sinai Peninsula to the West Bank. Israel also unified Jerusalem. As with the 1948 war, the 1967 war ended with an armistice, creating war heroes out of men like Yitzhak Rabin and Ariel Sharon.

Despite attempts to create peace after the Six Day War, the Arab nations refused to recognize Israel, and Israel refused to withdraw from any of the land it captured in 1967. After conquering the territories, Israel began encouraging Jewish settlement in the new territories, and in the 1970s, more than 10,000 Jews moved into the West Bank, Gaza Strip, Golan Heights, East Jerusalem, and the Sinai Peninsula, a figure that grew to over 100,000 by the early '80s and is now over 500,000 today. The loss of the Golan Heights has remained the foremost point of contention between Israel and Syria ever since, and its loss was never forgotten by Hafez, but before he could attempt to retake the Golan Heights, he would need to become president.

Hafez al-Assad took power in Syria much the same way others had done in the decades after French rule: a coup d'état. In February 1971, Assad led a military coup that made him the first Alawite president of Syria (Nisan 2002, 122), and with that the Alawite minority effectively held all the reigns of the Syrian government. Alawites were promoted in both the military and Ba'ath Party (Nisan 2002, 122), while Sunni military officers were often placed in less important positions and in distant regions (Faksh 1984, 145). This subsequently caused severe sectarian strife, and in the years immediately after Assad's seizure of power, he was often forced to walk a political tightrope.

The fact that Syria is ruled by a minority party is actually not an anomaly in the Middle East. The royal thrones in Jordan and Saudi Arabia are ruled by minority tribes, and the regime of Saddam Hussein in Iraq was comprised of both a tribal and religious minority in a state with a Shiite majority. (Nisan 2002, 125). However, when Hafez al-Assad came to power, he was still forced to walk a fine line between his Alawite background, the Arab nationalism of the Ba'ath Party, and the majority Sunni population. For instance, he openly opposed Zionism and Israel, which was popular with most Arabs no matter their sect, but he also supported Shia Persian Iran against Sunni Arab Iraq in the Iran-Iraq War during the 1980s (Nisan 2002, 126). To deflect criticism of his government as being dominated by a heretical sect, Assad made attempts to portray the Alawites as a mainstream Islamic sect, and in 1973, 80 leading members of the Alawite community issued a formal proclamation that they are true Muslims of the Shia branch and that they follow the Quran like other Muslims (Batatu 1981, 355). Assad himself appealed to Musa al-Sadr, a leading Shia cleric in Lebanon, and al-Sadr subsequently issued a *fatwa* that declared the Alawites to be legitimate Shia Muslims (Seale 1995, 173). Finally, Assad knew not to alienate influential urban Sunnis in Damascus who were less conservative, and he avoided doing that by bringing many of them into the Ba'ath Party (Faksh 1984, 142).

Although Assad's juggling act of making the Alawites appear mainstream while not alienating the majority Sunnis too much may have helped bring stability to his regime, he maintained power through the creation of a sophisticated police state apparatus that cemented his rule and continues to exist today under his son Bashar. Police states and dictatorships have long gone together, and it could be said that Hafez perfected the police state in Syria. One of the key aspects in Assad's successful use of the police state was that it was staffed with those loyal to the dictator, namely members of the Alawite sect and in particular the al-Assad family (Batatu 1981, 332). For example, Hafez's brother Rifaat was essentially his second-in-command and controlled between 12,000-25,000 defense forces that surrounded Damascus and all routes in and out of the city (Batatu 1981, 331). His other brother Jamil, and his cousin Adnan al-Assad, also controlled similar "defense" forces that were essentially there to defend the Assad regime (Batatu 1981, 331).

Despite Assad's employment of police state tactics in order to hold power over Syria, most of the people who remembered the years of instability before his reign were willing to give up some of their freedoms for security (Lesch 2012, 5), and Assad was also popular among large segments of Syrian society and the outside world for other perceived successes he had during his presidency. Most people who believe that Hafez al-Assad was a successful president generally point to four areas they believe he did well: Syria was able to take care of it resource needs; population control was dealt with; social systems were established; and a credible military was built (Zisser 2007, 108-9). That said, one should not be too quick to assign any or even all of these as victories for Hafez, because many of these same polices appear to have become a detriment to Bashar's rule; any policy that was considered successful must be viewed critically before it can be deemed beneficial in the long-term. For instance, the establishment of social systems in any country requires money or some type of resources in order for it to work, and the services are usually paid for from the taxes of the country's more wealthy citizens, which can come back to hurt the economy by leading to both a shrinking tax base and less spending by the most taxed. Likewise, in order to make a military formidable, public spending also requires taxes, which can lead to similar problems, all of which were experienced in Hafez's later rule and during much of Bashar's, as discussed in subsequent chapters.

Hafez was also seen as being successful in the realm of international affairs, but naturally, success in this area is both relative and subjective. After all, political success in a Western country, where governments are fairly stable, is quite different from success in a Middle Eastern country where turmoil is a common occurrence. Despite the almost constantly volatile situation in the Middle East, Assad usually acted in a reactive way to events and was noted for a lack of initiative, which was actually viewed by many as a strength (Zisser 2007, 3). Although he always towed a strong line against Israel, which included supporting anti-Israeli groups such as Hamas and Hezbollah, he also tried to make peaceful overtures to the West, most notably his country's participation in Operation Desert Storm in 1991 against Saddam Hussein's Iraq (Lesch 2012, 11).

Not surprisingly, international politics and affairs were never far from Hafez during his rule of Syria, particularly regarding Israel. Despite losing handily in the Six Day War to Israel, Syria and Egypt, which was led by Anwar al-Sadat after Nasser's death in 1970, plotted secretly to take back the lands they lost (Seale 1995, 190). In April 1973, Assad met with representatives from the Soviet Union and was able to acquire more than 100 state-of-the-art surface to air missile (SAM) batteries and at least 400 anti-aircraft guns (Seale 1995, 193).

Once the Arab forces were able to equip their armies with as much modern Soviet technology as possible, they launched a pre-emptive strike against Israeli forces in the Sinai Peninsula and the Golan Heights on October 6, 1973 (Seale 1995, 206). The war would last most of the month of October and since has since become known as the Yom Kippur War because it was launched during the Jewish holiday of Yom Kippur, also known as the Day of Atonement.

As soon as the war was initiated, there were cracks in the Arab coalition. After Sadat made modest gains into the Sinai he began to negotiate with the Israelis through American Secretary of State Henry Kissinger as proxy (Seale 1995, 208). The Israelis turned the tide within a week, and they launched a counteroffensive that won the war within 3 weeks. When the fighting ended, the national boundaries remained what they were after the 1967 war and any hopes the Arabs had in diplomatically gaining back lost territory was dashed once they realized that Kissinger and the United States – who served as intermediaries during the peace negotiations – were firmly on the side of Israel (Seale 1995, 215). The Egyptians under Sadat were eventually able to get the Sinai back, but this was only at the cost of many lives and after many years of negotiations.

Although Israel was winning the Yom Kippur War, the fact that the end result was technically a stalemate provided a moral victory for the Arabs on some level, since it proved they could fight toe to toe with the Israelis. However, Syria felt it lost through a peace process that was stacked against them. As Hafez al-Assad biographer Patrick Seale put it, "Sadat duped Assad and in turn was duped himself (Seale 1995, 215)." Hafez would never see the Golan Heights under Syrian rule.

In the years after the Yom Kippur War, Hafez al-Assad was engaged in another war that took place within the borders of Syria and was more of a threat to his rule and life than the Israelis ever were. The economic stability that Assad is often credited for bringing to Syria after he took power began to wane by the late 1970s, and because of this, many Syrians began to grow weary of Assad's nepotism and cronyism, both of which were rampant in the government (Seale 1995, 317). The economic woes were further compounded by Arab politics, as the oil rich Gulf States began to reduce the flow of oil to Syria as punishment for Assad's use of the Syrian military in Lebanon against Palestinians that were intent on massacring Christians (Seale 1995, 320). When economic problems begin to manifest themselves in a country, other social problems are usually not long in showing themselves as well, which in Syria often takes the form of sectarian conflict.

Hafez al-Assad's biggest battle did not come against Israel but against citizens of his own country. Tensions between his Alawite government and more fundamentalist elements of the Sunni population were always simmering, but in the late 1970s they boiled over, and on June 16, 1979 gunmen opened fire on cadets at the Aleppo Artillery School in northern Syria, killing as many as 83 (Seale 1995, 316). Alawites were disproportionately killed, and it was not long before the culprits were discovered to be members of the Muslim Brotherhood, an ultra-fundamentalist political organization that originated in Egypt (Seale 1995, 317). The Muslim Brotherhood had a litany of protests against Assad's government, which included the overwhelmingly Alawite character of the government – they considered the sect as apostates – and the secular stance of the Ba'ath Party (Faksh 1984, 147). The Muslim Brotherhood saw their largest areas of support in the cities of Aleppo, Damascus, and Hama, and these urban centers were centers of violence during the Muslim Brotherhood's campaign. For instance, from 1979-1981, the Muslim Brotherhood killed over 300 people in those cities, and most of their victims were Ba'ath Party members and Alawites. A number of Muslim clerics who denounced the violence were also executed (Seale 1995, 325).

Hafez's rule hinged on striking back against the Muslim Brotherhood, but before Assad was able to win his war against the Muslim Brotherhood, he suffered some setbacks that nearly cost him his life. In June 1980, would-be assassins from the Muslim Brotherhood fired machine guns and hurled grenades at Assad as he met an African visitor at the Guest Palace (Seale 1995, 328-29). Assad narrowly escaped with his life, and he reacted ruthlessly by having 500 imprisoned members of the Muslim Brotherhood summarily executed the next day. He also made membership in the organization a capital offense (Seale 1995, 329).

Assad also narrowly escaped another plot against his life by Sunni military officers in January 1982. In response to that attempted assassination, Assad's forces killed somewhere between 10,000-40,000 in the city of Hama by subjecting it to a military pounding (Nisan 2002, 127). Naturally, Assad loyalists claimed the enemy "pounced on our comrades while sleeping in their homes and killed whomever they could kill of women and children, mutilating the bodies of the martyrs in the streets, driven, like mad dogs, by their black hatred." Due to that, Assad's forces had to "confront these crimes" and teach the enemy "a lesson that has snuffed out their breath" However, Syrian journalist Subhi Hadidi described the carnage by writing that "under the command of General Ali Haydar, besieged the city for 27 days, bombarding it with heavy artillery and tank [fire], before invading it and killing 30,000 or 40,000 of the city's citizens – in addition to the 15,000 missing who have not been found to this day, and the 100,000 expelled."

The ruins of Hama

Although Assad narrowly escaped assassination twice, his sometime confidant and ally, Anwar al-Sadat of Egypt, was assassinated by members of the Muslim Brotherhood on October 6, 1981 (Seale 1995, 331). Sadat's assassination no doubt made Assad turn inwards and become more introspective, but it also appears to have made Assad much more brutal towards his enemies. The massacre of Hama was not the only such event perpetrated by Assad during his war with the Muslim Brotherhood. A large part of Hafez's success in his war against the Muslim Brotherhood can be attributed to the actions of his brother Rifaat, who was in charge of the campaign against the Muslim Brotherhood and used torture, intimidation, and other violent tactics to eventually fight them. While the Muslim Brotherhood was put down, Hafez was no longer viewed as a traditional Middle Eastern leader but as a cold and calculating modern despot.

Hafez and Rifaat (left)

This violent world of warring Islamic sects, an almost constant state of war with Israel, and continuous tension with the West was what Bashar al-Assad grew up in and learned about from an early age.

Chapter 4: Bashar al-Assad and the Syrian Presidency

"During its decades of rule... the Assad family developed a strong political safety net by firmly integrating the military into the government. In 1970, Hafez al-Assad, Bashar's father, seized power after rising through the ranks of the Syrian armed forces, during which time he established a network of loyal Alawites by installing them in key posts. In fact, the military, ruling elite, and ruthless secret police are so intertwined that it is now impossible to separate the Assad government from the security establishment.... So... the government and its loyal forces have been able to deter all but the most resolute and fearless oppositional activists. In this respect, the situation in Syria is to a certain degree comparable to Saddam Hussein's strong Sunni minority rule in Iraq." – Foreign Policy magazine editorial, 2011

When Bashar al-Assad was born on September 11, 1965, he became Hafez's third child with his first wife, and he never had any aspirations of ruling Syria or being in the military or Ba'ath Party as a young man. In fact, his dream was to be an ophthalmologist, and as a young adult he trained to be an ophthalmologist in London during the 1990s. According to Bashar himself, one of the reasons ophthalmology interested him is because there was a lack of blood. While there, he was noted by fellow students and his teachers (who all knew his family background) for his humble and almost austere lifestyle (Zisser 2007, 23). Bashar was described as likable by his classmates, but a bit quiet and not especially outgoing (Zisser 2007, 23).

As much as Bashar may have dreamed of being an ophthalmologist and helping his fellow Syrians with their eye problems, duty and fate would quickly propel the young Assad to power in Syria. On January 21, 1994, Bashar's brother Basil, who was the "heir apparent" to their father Hafez's presidency, was killed in a car accident in the Syrian capital of Damascus (Zisser 2007, 19). Basil's untimely death left the Assad patriarch in a quandary. Hafez had invested time and energy into making sure that Basil would be a proper replacement, but upon his son's death a new replacement had to be found. Bashar was chosen by his father as a replacement because he was the oldest surviving son – he was actually two years older than Basil – and seen as a viable candidate because of his education and intelligence. Although he had previously shown no interest in wielding power, Bashar began to be groomed to eventually take power, and he explained the sense of duty he felt to Syria in a 2013 interview with *Der Spiegel*, a German publication: "It's human to love where you come from. But it is not just a question of the emotional relationship. It is also about what you, as a person, can do for your home, especially when you are in a position of authority. That becomes especially clear in times of crisis."

At first, there were major obstacles to his assumption of power (Zisser 2007, 30). Bashar had no military experience and he was not a member of the Ba'ath Party, both of which effectively acted as the power behind the government. Also, Syria was at least nominally a republic, which meant that Bashar would have to be first "selected" (or sanctified) by the Ba'ath Party and then stand in a general election, even if that election was fraudulent. If Hafez did not follow the protocol, he would run the risk of being accused of being a potentate of the Saudi variety and risk falling in a putsch to the military and Ba'ath Party, the very people who put him in power. Thus, to counter-act any ill perception important peoples may have had about Hafez elevating Bashar as his heir apparent, Hafez placed his son in the army, where he made vital contacts and built his power base (Zisser 2007, 30).

Before he became president of Syria, Bashar also became involved in his own machinations that were intended to strengthen his power base. One of the most notable steps he took was marrying a Sunni woman, Asma, which no doubt helped him appear less sectarian and appeal to the Sunni majority (though the two had a relationship before he was ever made heir apparent to the Syrian presidency) (Zisser 2007, 63). Asma's beauty and Western roots were alluring to outsiders, as captured in a notorious profile of her done by *Vogue* magazine: "Asma al-Assad is glamorous, young, and very chic--the freshest and most magnetic of first ladies. Her style is not the couture-and-bling dazzle of Middle Eastern power but a deliberate lack of adornment. She's a rare combination: a thin, long-limbed beauty with a trained analytic mind who dresses with cunning understatement. Paris Match calls her 'the element of light in a country full of shadow zones.'"

Photo of Asma al-Assad taken by Ricardo Stuckert for Agência Brasil

Despite the overtures and alliances he and his dad made, some Syrians were not happy with Bashar becoming the face of their country. Hafez's once loyal brother, Rifaat, who was living in exile due to fallout between the two, was implicated in a plot to kill Bashar, and the Assad regime reacted by killing and imprisoning several of Rifaat's supporters in 1999, which stopped any threat he posed to Bashar (Zisser 2007, 37).

With alliances made and enemies eliminated the only obstacle left in the way for Bashar to become president was his father, until June 10, 2000, when Hafez died of a heart attack at the age of 69. Right away, machinations were underway to ensure Bashar became president. First, the constitution had to be changed to allow the 34 year old Bashar to assume office because the minimum age requirement was 40 (Zisser 2007, 39). One week after his father's death, on June 17, 2000, Bashar took the oath of loyalty that made him president of Syria after a fraudulent election was conducted, in which he won 97% of the vote (Zisser 2007, 41).

Despite the questionable election and tactics that placed him in Syria's highest office and the obvious specter of his father's brutally authoritarian reign, many in Syria and across the world viewed Bashar al-Assad with optimism. The optimism that many felt towards Bashar al-Assad was based on a combination of his age, educational background, and his physical looks. Bashar was viewed by many across the world as a bright young attractive leader who was married to an equally bright and attractive woman. In that regard, Asma was an important piece of the puzzle, as her Western ways not only attracted foreigners but also induced them to believe Syria might be on the path toward Westernization. As the *Vogue* magazine profile glowed, "The first lady works out of a small white building in a hilly, modern residential neighborhood called Muhajireen, where houses and apartments are crammed together and neighbors peer and wave from balconies. The first impression of Asma al-Assad is movement--a determined swath cut through space with a flash of red soles. Dark-brown eyes, wavy chin-length brown hair, long neck, an energetic grace. No watch, no jewelry apart from Chanel agates around her neck, not even a wedding ring, but fingernails lacquered a dark blue-green. She's breezy, conspiratorial, and fun. Her accent is English but not plummy. Despite what must be a killer IQ, she sometimes uses urban shorthand: 'I was, like…'"

Furthermore, Bashar did not fit the standard profile of a Middle Eastern despot. For example, he did not wear a military uniform replete with medals he never won, nor was he known for fiery invective that demonized Israel or the West. He was a young man that many had high hopes for, to the extent that even before he became the president many in Syria had nicknamed him "The Hope" (Lesch 2012, 2). Much of the high hopes for Bashar no doubt were the result of his age, but much of it was also the result of his own words and actions shortly after he became president. Assad announced that the central commitments of his presidency were the following: the continuity of his father's programs; modernization of Syrian society; more openness; and a more intellectual approach to the country's problems (Zisser 2007, 52-56). Bashar also made attempts, at least outwardly, to de-Ba'ath the government by limiting some of the party's powers (Zisser 2007, 73). In his own words, he suggested the direction that he intended to take the Syrian government:

> "Democracy is obligatory, but we must not enact the democracy of others. The Western democracies stemmed from a long history which produced leaders and traditions that created the present culture of democratic societies. We, by contrast, must adapt a democracy distinctive to us, founded on our history, culture and civilization and stemming from the needs of the society and reality in which we live." (Zisser 2007, 41)

Although what Bashar said concerning democracy and the development of his nation may be true, it's also easy to detect a slight tone of defiance in his words. Bashar's idea of Syrian democracy was continuous with his father's and essentially revolved upon the concept that what was good for the Assad family, the military, the Alawites, and the Ba'ath Party was good for Syria as a whole.

However, Bashar, like his father, would face many problems from the beginning of his rule, many of which were inherited from Hafez. As noted earlier, the economy that worked well in the first few years of Hafez al-Assad's reign as Syrian president gave way to stagnation by the late 1970s. In any society that experiences a period of economic vibrancy the social problems it has tend to be mitigated, while conversely periods of recession or depression often aggravate those same problems. In the case of Syria, when Bashar came to power, the economy itself was one of the major social problems. Syria's economy at the beginning of the new millennium was far from being modern and was for the most part archaic. For example, in 2000 there were no private banks in Syria, and most citizens did not use the national banks or own credit cards (Zisser 2007, 104). The lack of credit card use may be viewed by some as beneficial, but it is also is an example of the truly pre-modern condition the Syrian economy was in when Bashar became president. Along the same lines, there was only one ATM machine in the entire country and no stock market (Zisser 2007, 105). This was all the result of Ba'ath Party socialist economic policies, which were intended to promote equity and reduce corruption but in reality had the opposite effect, because corruption and a black market flourished and there was an almost total absence of domestic capital investment (Lesch 2012, 8). Bashar made attempts to liberalize the economy by allowing private banks and other domestic investment plans, all with limited success (Zisser 2007, 105-6).

The anemic economy that Bashar inherited from his father no doubt was a factor in his current problems, but Assad also carried on many of his father's same policies towards dissidents, which would later be a reason for many outside of Syria to oppose his regime. One of the major criticisms of the Hafez al-Assad regime was over his treatment of political rivals and dissidents. Hafez's brutal crackdown on the Muslim Brotherhood was crushing, but Bashar's suppression of dissidents may have been more insidious, and it began to hurt his image in the eyes of the outside world. Many Syrians initially believed that Bashar was a legitimate reformer who would lead his country towards a true democracy, so shortly after Bashar's assumption of the presidency, many politically minded Syrians began to form "cultural forums", which were essentially groups that met at various locations (including at members' homes) to discuss the problems facing their country and how best to solve them (Zisser 2007, 84). As the numbers of Syrians who participated in those forums grew, Assad and the Ba'ath Party carried out a three-pronged attack on these groups, who they began to view as dissidents and enemies (Zisser 2007, 89-92). First, many dissidents were physically assaulted, while others met with serious and "mysterious" accidents (Zisser 2007, 89). Next, leaders of the cultural forums were forced to obtain permits, which were often costly and nearly impossible to get, or risk fines and/or jail time (Zisser 2007, 90). Finally, writers of dissident publications were arrested (Zisser 2007, 90-92). Bashar tried to counteract any negative image he had acquired by these actions by releasing a number of other political dissidents who were imprisoned before this crackdown, but the political and social damage had been done (Zisser 2007, 93). The world began to view Bashar much as they did his father. Although Bashar was younger and more modern, his actions began to belie his true nature as a typical Middle Eastern despot.

If Bashar's reign as Syrian president began with difficulty because of the socio-economic situation inside Syria, events outside his country would make his rule even more difficult. On Bashar's 36th birthday, September 11, 2001, the United States was hit with the most devastating terrorist attacks in its history. Americans were angry and wanted retribution and justice for the lost lives of their countrymen, and President George W. Bush vowed to do everything in his power to destroy and/or capture those who were responsible, which included Osama bin-Laden, al-Qaeda, and the Taliban. Bush also included Syria as a member of the "Axis of Evil". Initially, Bashar attempted to use the United States' misfortune and anger to his advantage by cooperating with U.S. intelligence and giving them information on al-Qaeda, but as Zisser notes, this may have been done more because he feared another Islamic insurgency in Syria like that which his father faced 20 years earlier (Zisser 2007, 136). It has also been suggested that Assad was not as forthcoming about information on al-Qaeda as the Americans would have liked, which suggests that he was simply continuing his father's geopolitical legacy of playing both sides in struggles between the Western and Islamic worlds (Zisser 2007, 132).

Regardless of Assad's motives, U.S.-Syrian relations briefly experienced a détente after the 9-11 attacks, but this was dashed when the American "War on Terror" expanded to target neighboring Middle Eastern dictatorships. The U.S. invasion of Iraq in 2003 was an event that hurt Syria's economy and placed Bashar in the crosshairs of many American politicians. As noted earlier, Syria had supported the Shiite Persian Iranians in their war against the Sunni Arab Saddam Hussein regime in the 1980s, but after the Iran-Iraq War and the Cold War ended, alliances shifted and old enemies became new friends. Syria and Iraq normalized relations in 1997, and shortly thereafter the two nations began an economic policy through which Syria received cheap oil from their petroleum rich neighbor (Zisser 2007, 133). The U.S. invasion of Iraq not only stopped the flow of that cheap oil into Syria but also conceivably placed Assad into the same category as Saddam Hussein as a Cold War relic whose time had passed. Because of this, Bashar continued to support Hussein until he was captured, which further angered President Bush and several other American lawmakers (Zisser 2007, 127). After Hussein was captured and later executed, thousands of American soldiers began to occupy the Syrian-Iraqi border, which prompted Assad to make conciliatory gestures towards his political opponents in Syria. Assad's olive branch – whether real or just for show – was soundly rejected by most Syrians, who largely viewed it as an acquiescence towards growing American power in the region (Zisser 2007, 95).

Furthermore, it escaped nobody's notice that throughout the war in Iraq, Islamic jihadists were flooding across Syria's border with Iraq and joining the battle to fight American and other Western soldiers occupying the country and attempting to rebuild it.

Despite the position that the 9-11 attacks and the U.S. invasion of Iraq put Bashar in, he survived the first few years of his reign, and considering the political and cultural milieu he lived in, those years could be considered personally successful. However, pride comes before the fall, and Bashar's hubris soon put him on the path to where he finds himself today. When Bashar was re-elected to another seven year term through another dubious referendum, his self-satisfaction (or arrogance) was noticed by his biographer, respected journalist David Lesch (Lesch 2012, 31). Perhaps Assad felt more secure in his position as the American threat on his Iraqi border had dissipated by then; war-weary Americans who had tired of seeing many of their countrymen come home hurt or dead gave control of both houses of Congress to the Democrats in the 2006 mid-term elections. President Bush no longer had the political authority or the support of the American people to target other Middle Eastern countries.

All the while, the Bush administration distrusted Assad, and by the end of Bush's second term, the U.S. had no ambassador to Syria. As Bush put it in 2007, "My patience ran out on President Assad a long time ago. The reason why is because he houses Hamas, he facilitates Hezbollah, suiciders go from his country into Iraq, and he destabilises Lebanon." This was no doubt a reference to Syria's continued meddling in Lebanon, particularly its connections with Hezbollah. In the summer of 2006, the Shiite militia, based in southern Lebanon, launched hundreds of rockets at Israel and conducted a surprise cross-border raid that killed several Israeli soldiers. Israeli troops rushed into southern Lebanon, in the hopes of destroying Hezbollah, and the war in Lebanon lasted nearly 2 months, but Israel was unable to destroy Hezbollah, which managed to fire thousands of rockets indiscriminately into Israel, forcing Israelis in the north to all but live in bunkers during the war. The United Nations eventually brokered a ceasefire that called for stationing U.N. forces on the border to stand between Israel and Hezbollah, while also forbidding the shipment of weaponry from Iran and Syria into Lebanon. But the fighting indicated the extent to which Hezbollah, Hamas, Iran, and Syria were now all connected, posing grave security threats to Western interests. Despite the fact Hamas is an offshoot of the Muslim Brotherhood, the very group Bashar's father cracked down on decades earlier, the geopolitical situation made for strange bedfellows.

Chapter 5: The Arab Spring and Civil War

"First of all, you're talking about the president of the United States, not the president of Syria -- so he can only talk about his country. It is not legitimate for him to judge Syria. He doesn't have the right to tell the Syrian people who their president will be. Second, what he says doesn't have anything to do with the reality. He's been talking about the same thing -- that the president has to quit -- for a year and a half now. Has anything happened? Nothing has happened." – Bashar al-Assad

As part of his administration's efforts to reverse Bush's foreign policy, President Obama hoped to normalize relations with America's traditional Middle Eastern adversaries and engage with them. A new ambassador was appointed to Syria, and Secretary of State Hillary Clinton famously said of Assad, "There's a different leader in Syria now. Many of the members of Congress of both parties who have gone to Syria in recent months have said they believe he's a reformer." However, any pretense of Assad being a reformer would disappear quickly.

The Arab Spring officially began in December 2010 in Tunisia when a student and fruit vendor named Muhammad Bouazizi had his fruit cart confiscated by police who probably wanted a bribe (Lesch 2012, 45). Bouazizi reacted with the extreme form of protest of self-immolation, a suicide that led to protests fuelled by social media. The protests reached the capital of Tunis on January 13, 2011, and they ultimately forced Tunisia's dictator, Ben Ali, to flee to Saudi Arabia (Lesch 2012, 47).

The scene of angry street protests directed at a despotic leader was replayed in Egypt, and as the protests continued, Western pressure induced Egyptian dictator Hosni Mubarak to step down from the presidency just weeks after the events in Tunisia (Lesch 2012, 48). It seemed that no dictator in the Arabic speaking world was immune, and protests sprouted from the Gulf States to Morocco. Despots who had ruled for decades, including Ali, Mubarak, and Qaddafi in Libya, were eventually overthrown.

Although Syria witnessed anti-government protests similar to those in other countries during the Arab Spring, they were initially much smaller and not very organized (Lesch 2012, 53). The lack of large-scale protests initially in Syria can be attributed to its uniqueness as a nation among its Arabic speaking neighbors. The complex intelligence and police state apparatus in Syria no doubt contributed to stamping out many of the protests before they could grow into something much larger, but the personality and public perception of Bashar al-Assad is another factor that mitigated protests in Syria. Bashar was much less hated by his people than the other dictators who were toppled during the Arab Spring (Lesch 2012, 52). For example, Ali and Mubarak were viewed by many of their peoples as American stooges, while Qaddafi had rightly earned his reputation as an eccentric tyrant.

One of the more important and unique aspects of Syria that reduced the amount and intensity of initial protests there was its demographic composition. In the 21st century, Syria is a country comprised of many different religious sects and tribes; the Sunni Muslims are the majority, but the minority Shia and Christian sects form about 30% of the population, and they have traditionally been loyal to the al-Assad family, who they view as protectors (Lesch 2012, 51-52).

As the last two years have made clear, far worse has happened in Syria than mere protests. If the early Arab Spring protests never took hold in Syria, how did the country devolve into the current situation? The answer is a combination of Assad's hubris and his inability to understand tide of change in the Middle East. It is unknown whether or not if the protests would have been suppressed or fizzled out, but in March 2011, several schoolboys from the southwestern Syrian city of Deraa scribbled the words "down with the regime" in Arabic on a wall in their school (Lesch 2012, 55). In any other time the boys would have probably just been punished by the school authorities, but in the shadow of the Arab Spring the kids were arrested and tortured (Lesch 2012, 56). As a result of the children's incarceration and torture, their families protested in central Deraa on March 15, 2011, which then spread across Syria via social networking websites (Lesch 2012, 56). Ironically, these repressive tactics were being used the very same month *Vogue*'s puff piece on Asma was published, making clear the extent of the Assad family's propaganda attempts with the West and humiliating the magazine so badly that the article on Asma was quickly removed from their website. As Gawker's editor, John Cook, put it, "I think it's important that people are aware of how Vogue…felt about the Assads, and characterized the Assads. It came out almost exactly as the regime embarked on its campaign of murdering women and children…And now in the context of the United States possibly going to war with Syria, it's important for people to see how the magazine portrayed them… "

Bashar might have been able to stem the tide of the protests with conciliatory gestures, but his pride and ego got the best of him. Instead of admitting the mistakes his police agents made in the Deraa situation, Assad chose to blame outside sources and "conspiracies" for the protests and unrest. Bashar said in a speech to the Syrian People's Assembly on March 30, 2011: "Our enemies work every day in an organized, systemic and scientific manner in order to undermine Syria's stability. We acknowledge that they had been smart in choosing very sophisticated tools in what they have done, but at the same time we realize that they have been stupid in choosing this country and this people, for such conspiracies do not work with our country or our people." (Lesch 2012, 76-77) Even late in 2012, with the civil war raging, Assad remained defiant when *Der Spiegel* asked if he was sorry about the way his supporters handled Deraa: "There were personal mistakes made by individuals. We all make mistakes. Even a president makes mistakes. But even if there were mistakes in the implementation, our decisions were still fundamentally the right ones."

Bashar's obstinate attitude toward the protesters took a violent turn when he gave his brother, Maher, a free hand to deal with them. Maher filled a role similar to Hafez's brother Rifaat before he was exiled from Syria, as he was head of the Fourth Armored Division and the Republican Guard, which served to protect the regime (Lesch 2012, 105). Just as Hafez called in Rifaat to put down the Muslim Brotherhood insurgency in the late 1970's and early 1980s, Bashar appealed to Maher to suppress protests in Syria 30 years later, which he gladly did with equally brutal methods, often carried out personally (Lesch 2012, 105). The primary difference between the two situations was that the methods employed by Hafez and Rifaat ultimately proved to be successful, while those used by Bashar and Maher have apparently thrown Syria into a state of sectarian warfare.

One of the primary strengths of the Assad dynasty, the backing of the Alawite sect, also became one of the major reasons why Syria devolved into sectarian warfare. Most of the government and police forces who participated in the violent crackdowns against protesters were Alawites, while the majority of the opposition was from the Sunni community, which was portrayed by the Assad regime as fundamentalists (Lesch 2012, 106). Assad has used the fragmented sectarian demographic background of Syria to his advantage by arguing that if fundamentalist Sunnis came to power in Syria, it would mean bloodshed for the Alawites, Ishmailis, Druze, and Christians whom his family protected. After all, the Syrian minorities only needed to look at the persecution the Christian Copts of Egypt were experiencing in the wake of their Arab Spring (Lesch 2012, 107).

Although Assad's tactic of dividing Syria's population may have initially helped him stay in power, it had the effect of deepening the sectarian conflict. Furthermore, as defectors from the Syrian army began to form the Free Syrian Army, Islamic militant jihadists also began to enter the war (Lesch 2012, 174-75). Although the Free Syrian Army is comprised of a lot of secular elements (British Broadcasting Company 2013, October 17), Assad's propaganda campaign has tirelessly depicted his enemies as al-Qaeda connected terrorists, and he has portrayed a potential Free Syrian Army victory as genocide for Syria's Shia and Christian communities. The fear has prompted paramilitary Alawite gangs, known as *Shabihas* (ghosts in Arabic), to kill members of the opposition and Sunnis indiscriminately (Lesch 2012, 177). The situation in Syria has effectively evolved over the last nearly three years from one of protest to revolution and now finally to a sectarian civil war that shows no signs of ending. Perhaps not surprisingly, Assad has denied the Shabihas exist, even while justifying their existence: "There is nothing called 'Shabiha' in Syria. In many remote areas where there is no possibility for the army and police to go and rescue the people and defend them, people have bought arms and set up their own small forces to defend themselves against attacks by militants. Some of them have fought with the army, that's true. But they are not militias that have been created to support the president. At issue is their country, which they want to defend from al-Qaida."

Assad's branding of his enemies as foreign agents and terrorists has greatly helped him. In response to questions from *Der Spiegel* about the Syrian people wanting him gone, Assad said of his enemies, "Again, when you talk about factions, whether they are opposition or supporters, you have to ask yourself the question: Whom do they represent? Themselves or the country that made them? Are they speaking for the United States, the United Kingdom, France, Saudi Arabia and Qatar? My answer here has to be frank and straight to the point. This conflict has been brought to our country from abroad. These people are located abroad, they live in five-star hotels and they say and do what those countries tell them to do. But they have no grassroots in Syria." At the same time, he has cast his opponents as the very al-Qaeda terrorists the West despises: "The whole problem wasn't about the president. What do killing innocents, explosions and the terrorism that al-Qaida is bringing to the country have to do with me being in office?"

The Western nations and the United Nations have not been able to reach a consensus on what steps to take regarding Assad and Syria, in part because Russia has long been a trade partner of Syria's, and the Russians want him to stay in power. Furthermore, Syria is a crucial bridge between Iran, Hezbollah, and Hamas. Iran had long been considered one of the world's largest state sponsors of terrorism against Western targets, but Iran became one of the West's foremost adversaries through the strengthening of its alliance with Syria; as Iran and Syria grew closer, Shiite Iran began to cultivate close ties with Hezbollah, a Shiite-dominated group that had always been a Syrian client. As Assad has fought a mixture of radical Islamists and Western backed moderates, Iran has provided assistance and Hezbollah soldiers have actually left Lebanon to fight on the ground in Syria.

Predicting the future is a difficult enterprise, but reasonable inferences about the course of Syria's civil war can be made based on the past. First, it does not appear that Assad will step down from the presidency under his own volition. The time for Assad to have stepped down without, or at least limited, repercussions would have been in August 2011, when the leaders of the United States and the European Union called on him to step down. Despite all kinds of calls for Assad to step down and leave the country, he has not only refused to leave but has remained defiant. In a late 2012 interview, he mocked Obama's calls for him to give up power: "First of all, you're talking about the president of the United States, not the president of Syria -- so he can only talk about his country. It is not legitimate for him to judge Syria. He doesn't have the right to tell the Syrian people who their president will be. Second, what he says doesn't have anything to do with the reality. He's been talking about the same thing -- that the president has to quit -- for a year and a half now. Has anything happened? Nothing has happened."

Since Assad refused to leave, as Lesch wrote, "there seemed to be no turning back for any of the principal parties involved (Lesch 2012, 164)." The stakes are too high for Assad at this point. If he peaceably steps down, the recent allegations that he used chemical weapons would almost ensure that he will be tried for war crimes in an international tribunal at The Hague or another place. It also appears that the time for Assad to reach a peaceful solution with the various factions in his own country has long since passed.

Today, it appears that the sectarian war in Syria will continue indefinitely, with two possible outcomes. It's possible the country may eventually be partitioned according to religious and ethnic affiliations, similar to the situation in India after it was given independence by Great Britain in 1947, but the more grim possibility is that the war spills over Syria's borders and becomes regional. Many different nations have competing interests and preferences regarding the outcome of Syria's civil war, and several of them are taking proactive steps to influence events, including Russia, Iran, Turkey, and Saudi Arabia.

Either way it appears that the war will continue for some time into the future and countless more lives will be lost before it is resolved. The house of cards that is Bashar al-Assad's presidency may fall, but if so, it will be in a manner that is slow and painful for all involved.

Bibliography

Aflaq, Michel. 1962. Nationalism and revolution. In Haim 1962. 242-251.

Batatu, Hanna. 1981. Some observations on the social roots of Syria's ruling, military group and the causes for its dominance. *Middle East Journal* 35: 331-344.

British Broadcasting Company. 2013. Syria crisis: Guide to armed and political opposition. October 17. http://www.bbc.co.uk/news/world-middle-east-24403003 [accessed on November 5, 2013].

———. 2013. Syria chemical weapons equipment destroyed, says OPCW. October 31. http://www.bbc.co.uk/news/world-middle-east-24754460 [accessed on November 5, 2013].

Dawisha, Adeed. 2003. *Arab nationalism: From triumph to despair*. Princeton: Princeton University Press.

Devlin, John F. 1976. *The Ba'th Party: A history from its origins to 1966*. Stanford, California: Hoover Institute Press.

Faksh, Mahmud A. 1984. The Alawi community of Syria: A new dominant political force. *Middle Eastern Studies* 20: 133-153.

Gellner, Ernest. 1983. *Nations and nationalism*. Ithaca: Cornell University Press.

Haim, Sylvia G., ed. 1962. *Arab nationalism: An anthology*. Los Angeles: University of California Press.

Lesch, David W. 2012. *Syria: The fall of the house of Assad*. New Haven: Yale University Press.

Nasser, Gamal Abdel. 1962. The philosophy of the revolution. In Haim 1962, 229-232.

Nisan, Mordechai. 2002. *Minorities in the Middle East: A history of struggle and self-expression*. 2nd ed. Jefferson, North Carolina: McFarland and Company.

The Party of the Arab Ba'th. 1962. Ba'ath Party Constitution. In Haim 1962, 233-241.

Seale, Patrick. 1995. *Assad of Syria: The struggle for the Middle East*. Revised ed. Los Angeles: University of California Press.

TREND News Agency. 2013. U.S., Russia agree on Syria U.N. chemical arms measure. September 27. http://en.trend.az/ [accessed October 3, 2013].

Watenpaugh, Keith David. 2006. *Being modern in the Middle East: Revolution, nationalism, colonialism, and the Arab middle class*. Princeton: Princeton University Press.

Wright, Edmund, ed. 2006. *A dictionary of world history*. 2nd ed. Oxford: Oxford University Press.

Zisser, Eyal. 2007. *Commanding Syria: Bashar al-Assad and the first years in power*. London: I.B. Tauris.

Printed in Great Britain
by Amazon